# ALLOWANCE MAGIC

## TURN YOUR KIDS INTO MONEY WIZARDS

**by David McCurrach**

Allowances are old news. Chances are you had one as a kid and your kids get one. Most parents give $5 a week and tell their children to spend it as they please. That's that. Little ventured, little gained.

What many parents don't realize is the magic an allowance program can perform. It can turn your kids into money wizards by teaching them to plan their expenditures and live within that plan. They learn to shop for value as well as compare price and quality. They also develop the habits of saving and sharing.

At the same time, allowances work their magic on the parent-child relationship. Arguments and stress associated with parents making all their kids' financial decisions are virtually eliminated. Open and honest communications are fostered. Mutual respect grows.

You can use *Allowance Magic* to teach your children about money and money management while helping them develop financial responsibility. In the process, you will greatly improve your relationship with your children and even save

*give your kids the money, along with the responsibility*

that $5 a week. How's that for some real money magic?

## The Magic

### Costs Less

And, as amazing as it sounds, it won't cost you any more money than what you're already spending. In fact, for most parents it ends up costing less. Kids tend to nickel and dime you to death with $10 for a movie, $7 for pizza, $5 for a game and $3 for a snack. When you see you're already spending $30 a week, a $20 allowance sounds like a bargain. Especially when it eliminates the repeated requests of $5 for this and $2 for that.

With *Allowance Magic,* you simply give your kids the money you're already spending on them along with the responsibility to make those purchases. In other words, if you're forking over $3 a week for snacks, $5 for a video and $2 for trading cards, you would give them a $10 weekly allowance and tell them if they want to buy a snack, rent a movie or get some trading cards, they need to use their own

money. When they ask you for $1 for a soda, you simply remind them their snacks are included in their allowance.

### Works Better

Not surprisingly, some parents don't stop there. They think they can also use the allowance to get household chores done or to get their kids to work harder in school. They don't look at it as bribes, but rather as paying for work. Unfortunately, it really doesn't matter how you look at it, because, over time, it just doesn't work.

You don't want your kids to say "I don't need the money this week, so I'm not making my bed" or "I'm not going to work hard on that course because $50 for an A is just not worth the effort." The bed needs to be made and the effort needs to be put forth.

You expect them to do their chores because they are responsible family members and everyone helps out around the house. You hope they do their homework because they get satisfaction from doing well in school and they realize how important school success is to their future achievements in college and career. Money shouldn't be a factor.

The consequence for not doing a chore needs to be the loss of a privilege. The consequence for a poor mark needs to be more study time. The threat of withholding money is not an effective motivator. The real magic of an allowance is to make your kids money-wise and financially responsible. Don't forsake the promise of the one for the futility of the other and end up accomplishing neither.

At the same time, don't hesitate to pay your kids for extra jobs around the house. Most kids jump at the chance to make money. If you'd consider paying someone else to cut your grass, weed your garden, shovel your walk or wash your car, go ahead and give your kids a chance to earn that extra cash. The same goes for helping with your business. Few people would consider filing papers or entering data into a computer in the same category as household chores. Being able to work and earn money at a young age gives your kids an even better opportunity to learn to manage money.

## Kids Learn

There are many things in life too dangerous, complex or far removed for kids to learn through their own experience. That's why we have thousands of textbooks and send children to school for most of their young lives. At the same time, there's no more effective teacher than real-world experience. Lessons learned through their own experiences as children can leave a life-long impression on them in terms of the habits they develop and the attitudes they form.

Money management is one of the things we learn primarily on our own. When we learn something in school, we all come away with about the same level of knowledge. Learning on our own means there are those who are exposed to a great deal of information and those who get none at all. That's why some people are so much better at money management than others. Many parents think this is something their kids can learn when they're out on their own and need to know it. And, of course, they can. Unfortunately, those lessons can be quite painful and costly.

What most parents don't realize is their children can easily and inexpensively start learning these lessons at a surprisingly young age. Teaching kids to manage money and helping them develop sound financial habits are opportunities few parents can afford to miss. The fact kids are able to grasp money concepts much earlier through their own real-life adventures than in the abstract world of school is just that much more reason to start early.

The lessons they learn and habits they develop as children are invaluable when they come face-to-face with the much more complex financial challenges of adulthood. Learning through their own experiences, guided by the shepherding hands of their parents, is the magic of allowances. That's how they become money wizards.

## Parents Relax

When you control your children's spending, you assume all responsibility for deciding what to buy and what not to buy. You make those decisions one purchase at a time. For instance, when your child wants to buy a shirt, you weigh all the factors surrounding the purchase:

- Is this shirt needed?
- Is this particular shirt the one to buy?
- Is this a good price?
- Can I afford it?
- And so on.

In addition to being demanding on the parents, these decisions are often unpopular with the kids. They can cause tension and even hostility between parents and children. That same decision, made by the kids themselves, is readily accepted and produces no conflict whatsoever.

With *Allowance Magic*, you decide how much money your children get and what it covers. They decide how to spend it. In the process, the successes and mistakes they experience help develop and refine their decision-making skills.

the successes and mistakes they experience help develop and refine their decision-making skills

This approach also limits how much you spend on them. When the parent maintains control over every nickel and dime, children often feel the amount of money available is unlimited. Granted, getting money may be a challenge, but the struggle is more than worth the effort. Especially when the children believe the parents have the funds for almost anything they could want.

Letting your children make their own financial decisions involves giving up a certain amount of parental control. This is control you're going to have to give up anyway as your kids get older. Why not do it now, when there's something in it for both of you?

The money and misery it saves can be substantial. Children's financial mistakes have little impact on their parents. Making those mistakes as adults can be extremely costly and difficult for parents and children alike. Which would you rather have your kids experience—small mistakes now or big mistakes later?

Finally, *Allowance Magic* improves communications. It gives you something meaningful to talk about with your children—something both of you feel is important. The process of changing your children's attitudes from the confrontational "You have money and I want it" to the self-assured "I've got money and I'm responsible with it" requires a good deal of honest and open communication. Resolving money conflicts this way can set the stage to resolve other areas of conflict in a similar fashion.

Does this sound like something you'd like to do, but don't know where to start? Relax. That's why we've written this book and *Journal*. Simply work through them one page at a time. When you're done, you may even impress yourself with your *Allowance Magic*.

# The Allowances

As you can imagine, this kind of magic doesn't just happen. It takes planning and preparation. Fortunately, the time and the effort required are minimal.

If you're a single parent, please overlook our references to "you and your spouse" and to "Mom and Dad."

As you read on, you'll see that two-parent households present additional challenges that need to be addressed. Most of these do not create a problem for a single parent. However, if you're unsure about any of your decisions or just need someone to bounce your ideas off, you may want to discuss this information with a trusted friend or close relative.

The first step is for parents to sit down by themselves and make sure they're on the same page. You and your spouse may have very different attitudes towards money and on how you teach your kids about money. Since less than half of all parents give allowances, the chances are good one of you got an allowance as a child and the other didn't. Even if you were the lucky one, your allowance was likely a giveaway—here's five bucks—or a bribe—$1 if you make your bed or $20 if you get an A. Neither approach is going to help your kids learn to manage money. If you really want them to become Money Wizards, you'll need to put your childhood experiences behind you and begin with a clean slate.

## The Potion

As you read on, you'll see you have a number of decisions to make. Collectively, they formulate The Potion you use to create your very own *Allowance Magic*. Your potion is a unique combination of allowance features and responsibilities. The exact formulation varies from family to family and from child to child. It takes into account your values as well as the individual needs and capabilities of each of your children.

This book uses an easy to understand, one step at a time approach to present all the information you need to develop the perfect potion. As you make each decision, you are directed to record it in THE POTION on page J14. Once that page is complete, it's time to stand back and let the magic begin!

We've marked each decision point with a beaker icon. We call them POTION POINTS. Next to each of these, we give a concise statement of exactly what needs to be decided at that point. When you've worked your way through all the POTION POINTS, you have the perfect potion for your family.

Give each decision serious consideration. Discuss each one thoroughly. Make sure you're comfortable with what you decide. Try to get it right the first time. Making frequent changes down the road can damage your credibility and lessen the effectiveness of your program.

Keep in mind, the benefits of this program result from letting your kids make their own spending decisions. The structure you establish lets them know there's a limit to the amount you give them to spend. The process allows them to learn to plan those expenditures, live within that plan, save for expensive items, share with others and become financially responsible.

After you complete this section, you will sit down with your children and determine how much you're already spending on them and which expenditures they can begin to handle themselves. But first, there are some basic decisions you and your spouse need to agree on. By taking a few minutes to discuss the following, you can be assured you'll present a united front to your child.

## Say What?

Children's financial needs generally fall into the following categories:

- Spending
- Saving
- Sharing
- Gifts
- Clothes

You're probably already spending money in each of these areas. Depending on your children's ages, they should be able to take responsibility for most, if not all, of these expenditures. At this point, you need to decide if and to what extent you'll let them handle each area. The following information will help you make those decisions.

*developing the saving habit as children makes their lives as adults much more manageable and rewarding*

***Spending***—The spending portion replaces the day-to-day dole you provide your kids for snacks, CDs, toys and the like. Rather than giving them $2 for this and $5 for that, you give them a predetermined amount and let them decide whether or not they'd rather spend the money on a snack today or go to a movie this weekend.

***Saving***—Saving is generally a lost art for kids and parents alike. Living in a world of instant gratification and easy credit makes the whole idea of saving foreign to most people. Kids who do not save never experience the anticipation and excitement that builds as they close in on a Saving Goal. They never know the pride that comes with the purchase and possession of something they bought with their own money. Even more tragic is the financial havoc not saving can create for them as adults.

Saving helps kids learn to pay themselves first and to get in the habit of planning for their future needs by setting aside a certain percentage of everything they make. It allows them to make larger purchases and cover major expenses. They learn that having 5 or 10% less to spend now is hardly noticeable while eventually having the money to buy a game system or their first car is something they'll never forget. Developing the saving habit as children makes their lives as adults much more manageable and rewarding.

***Sharing***—Learning they can make a difference in other people's lives through sharing their time and money is another lesson children can experience when they're young. It's a habit that will benefit them throughout their lives. Providing your kids money to share—a set amount for them to contribute to those less fortunate and to causes they believe in—gives them a feeling of worth no amount of spending can ever provide.

Sharing can also be therapeutic for kids. Maybe a family member is struggling with cancer and your kids find a donation to the Cancer Society makes them feel like they're doing something to help. Or maybe their favorite pet ran away and they find a donation to the local pet shelter eases some of the pain. Through sharing, they learn that sometimes the best way to help themselves is to help someone else.

*Gifts*—Don't confuse Sharing with giving presents. Gift giving is a sign of friendship and love. Chances are you now give your kids money to buy presents. For most families, it works just like any other kind of spending. They ask, you decide. With a Gift Allowance, you limit the amount you provide. If they want to spend more, they come up with it. It teaches your kids to plan their spending and to live within that plan. In the process, they learn to make much more reasonable gift decisions.

*Clothes*—Clothes spending can be a battle royale for families. The potential conflicts are huge. Chances are your kids see $60 for a pair of jeans as no big deal. After all, funds are unlimited and everyone's wearing that brand. You, on the other hand, feel the no-name pair at $20 is just fine. Or maybe that clearance-priced paisley top suits you, while your child thinks a more costly plain top is much more striking.

While you think you're controlling the spending, your child is busy learning how to manipu-

late you. You may feel once you get home from a shopping trip, it will be months before you'll be buying more clothes. Your child, on the other hand, may be planning to hit you up next week for those shoes you wouldn't buy today.

All this hassle is magically avoided with a Clothes Allowance. You give your children responsibility for making appropriate spending decisions within the allowance limit. They learn if they spend all their money on jeans they won't have enough for shirts. You avoid the endless requests for the latest fashion.

As you're formulating your plans, be cautious about combining needs and wants in the same allowance. You wouldn't like your kids to sacrifice needs to pursue wants. If you're concerned about excessive spending for a particular need, set up a separate allowance. For example, if your child is spending $10 a day on school lunches and you feel $3 is adequate, give them a $3 a day lunch allowance. If you're tempted to make it part of the Spending Allowance, consider the possibility of your kids skipping lunch to use the money to buy trading cards. Most parents don't want to give their kids that kind of option. We've provided some blank lines in THE POTION'S table of allowances for just such needs.

You also don't want your kids to use their allowances to buy inappropriate items. Don't be lured

into thinking because you're allowing them to spend their money as they please, you don't need to monitor what they buy. There are still limits and for *Allowance Magic* to be most effective, your kids need to stick to their Spending Plan (which should always be subject to parental review).

Please note that, in the pages that follow, we refer to the combined Spending, Saving and Sharing Allowance as either the "weekly allowance" or the "regular allowance".

## Say When?

The age you start any of these allowances depends on the ability of your children to begin to assume responsibility for each type of expenditure. This varies from child to child. In addition, you generally start young children with very limited responsibilities within each area and add more responsibilities as your children get older. Typically, they are able to assume some responsibilities for:

- Spending—Age 3
- Saving—Age 5
- Sharing—Age 5
- Gifts—Age 7
- Clothes—Age 9

Don't use these ages as an absolute guide. Think of them more as an indication of when you may want to consider giving additional allowances.

Decide right now which of these allowances you're ready to give your child. For your convenience, THE POTION, on page J14, includes a table listing various options. Indicate your decisions there.

> don't be lured into thinking you don't need to monitor what they buy

## Say How Often?

How often you give allowances depends on the nature of the allowance and the stage of your children's development. A teenager can easily plan their expenditures and manage their money over the period of a month. A 3-year-old, on the other hand, can only handle a day or two at a time. It's not uncommon to start with a daily allowance and end up with a monthly allowance.

Another consideration is the type of allowance. The regular allowance, which includes Spending, Saving and Sharing, is most commonly given on a weekly basis. The Clothes Allowance is typically given twice a year and the Gift Allowance is given on an as needed basis.

 Decide right now how often you will give each allowance to your child. Add your decision to THE POTION on page J14.

## Say How Much?

The Spending and Clothes amounts are based on how much money you're already giving your kids for those expenditures. The worksheets in the *Kid's Money Wizard Journal* give you the information you need to make these decisions. As your kids complete the worksheets, they learn to think about and plan their expenditures much in the same way adults do their spending.

Gifts are simply your decision.

Many parents provide a different amount for friend's gifts than for gifts to family members (say $5 for friends and $10 for family). This allowance represents the most you provide. If a particular gift costs less than the allowance amount, you would give no more than needed to purchase that item.

The Saving and Sharing amounts are generally based on a percentage of the weekly allowance (typically 5 or 10% each). This is much the same method adults use to come up with their Saving and Sharing amounts.

Decide right now how much you'll give for a Gift Allowance and what percentage you'll use for the Saving and Sharing Allowances. Add your decisions to THE POTION on page J14.

## Match This

Sometimes saving benefits from a little extra encouragement. Children commonly feel their goals are unattainable and their efforts inadequate. You may need to help them a little. Consider matching anything they save. It could be as generous as if you save $2,500 for a car, we'll give you another $2,500; or, as limited as if you save $12 for that game, we'll give you the other $12. You may want to present the idea as interest on savings. If so, you can use this opportunity to show them how long it takes to dou-

**no personal finance book would ever encourage a responsible individual to borrow in order to spend**

ble their money in a bank or credit union account.

Many parents don't feel it's appropriate to match the Saving Allowance amount. They choose to only match savings from spending money and extra earnings. Other parents look at matching the Saving Allowance amount as an extra encouragement to save.

Decide right now whether or not you're going to match Savings and if so, from what source and at what rate. For your convenience, THE POTION includes a table listing various options. Indicate your decisions there.

## No Slight of Hand

As your kids become better money managers, they will undoubtedly recognize the opportunity to help their savings with some of their Sharing money or beef up their spending with some of their savings. Many parents allow transfers into Saving and Sharing but not out.

Decide right now which transfers you're going to allow. For your convenience, THE POTION includes a table listing various options. Indicate your decisions there.

## Neither a Borrower Nor a Lender Be

Asking for an advance on an allowance is probably inevitable. It's your child's first brush with borrowing. Needless to say, no personal finance book would ever encourage a responsible individual to borrow in order to spend. Borrowing is generally limited to starting a business, making an investment and getting an education. Popular exceptions are made for homes and cars. Anything else spells disaster. Since your children probably don't want the advance to start a business, make an investment, pay for college or buy a home or car, you may not want to give it to them.

 Decide right now whether you're going to give advances on future allowances. Add your decision to THE POTION.

## Keep It Current

Your children's financial needs change as often as their shoe size. At the same time, their ability to earn extra money grows as fast as they do. A periodic review of the allowance amounts in terms of their needs and their capacity to meet those needs, as well as the frequency and types of allowances they receive, is helpful. This review will generally come less often as they get older (as will the frequency of the allowances themselves).

For younger children, it may be appropriate to sit down and review their allowances every couple of months. Older kids probably only need to do it once a year. Start each review with a new *Allowance Magic* book. Reread the material, revisit your decisions and rework the worksheets to reflect your child's current capacity to manage their own money. Be sure to also reevalu-ate the review frequency itself.

 Decide right now when you're going to have the next allowance review. Add your decision to THE POTION.

Rereading and reworking *Allowance Magic* assures you address your children's ever changing abilities to assume more and more financial responsibilities in terms of both expenditures and income. It also helps you recommit to the challenge and sharpen your focus on providing your children a first-rate financial education.

## Count Earnings

As soon as your kids are earning money on a regular basis from jobs like yard care and babysitting, they can begin to cover some of their own expenses. Hopefully, you've been encouraging them to save and share a portion of the money they earn, just as they do with the weekly allowance you give them.

*encourage them to save and share a portion of the money they earn*

You may want to start by only using a portion of their earnings to cover expenses. For example, if they make $20 a week babysitting, you may suggest they save $2, share $2 and reduce their $30 a week allowance by $10. Using all their money may discourage them from working.

Many parents use these earnings to first reduce and eventually eliminate the weekly allowance, followed by the Gift Allowance and ultimately the Clothes Allowance. Generally,

this is a slow process that takes place over a number of years. The idea is to get your kids in the habit of managing their allowance money and have those habits and skills carry over to the money they earn. Making that transition under the watchful eyes of Mom and Dad gives you a chance to smooth out any rough spots your kids may encounter before they are totally on their own.

## Put It In Writing

Writing down the amount of each allowance and exactly what it's intended to cover lessens misunderstandings and encourages cooperation. The *Kid's Money Wizard Journal* is designed to help you develop an effective allowance program as well as provide a record of the agreements between you and your children. When there's a question of who pays for what, pull out your *Journal* and settle it right away. You may also want to save old copies as a measure of your children's progress and as a keepsake of their financial development.

## Make a Commitment

To be of any lasting value, you need to stick to the program. There will be no *Allowance Magic* if you forget to pay the allowance or start paying for items covered by the allowance.

This is a proven program. It has helped thousands. Give it a chance to do its magic on your family. You may need to come up with a way to help you remember to pay the allowance. Some parents pay it every Sunday. This also helps your children avoid spending all their money over the weekend and not having any left for the rest of the week.

Don't be tempted to break your

own rules. If you want to make an exception, first discuss it with your spouse and agree on it. Then, go over it with your children. Make that exception part of your program.

## You're It

When your children are young, you are their primary source of funds. As they grow older, work they do for neighbors and relatives provides more money. Once they are old enough to take a part-time job, they can earn almost all the cash they need. For now, most, if not all, the money is coming from you.

You're also your kids' primary source of guidance. The *Kid's Money Wizard Journal* includes tips to help your kids refine their money management skills and develop beneficial financial habits. We call these tips The Challenges.

You may have additional ideas you feel would be helpful to your children's development. Each of the allowance areas has spaces for you to add your own suggestions on specific things your kids can do to become better money managers in that area. Read each section. Discuss it with your spouse. Write in any additional ideas you may have before you go over each area with your children.

## Be Lavish With Your Praise

Criticism, scolding and lecturing your kids on their mistakes is not the guidance they need to become better money managers. You may think you're helping them by pointing out each and every mistake. Maybe, you're concerned they don't realize they've made a mistake. Or possibly, you think they don't realize how

big a mistake it really was.

Trust us. They don't need this kind of help. They'll probably take your comments as criticism and feel either angry or helpless. At that point, the value of the lesson is lost. Your kids need a certain level of independence to be able to truly learn from their own experience. This includes freedom from criticism.

Praise has always been a much better motivator. Put your efforts into complimenting them on their successes. If they make a mistake, let them deal with the problems it creates themselves. That's how they learn. When they have a success, be lavish with your praise.

## You're Ready

Once you and your spouse have read and discussed the entire book, you're ready to sit down with your children and work the *Kid's Money Wizard Journal* together. Each section includes a series of challenges and many also have worksheets. Your children must master The Challenges to become Money Wizards. The worksheets help them plan each aspect of money management and help you determine the appropriate allowance amounts and financial responsibilities. The Potion has all the information you need to put your allowance program into action.

1.    Start by going over the allowances you'll give and the frequencies of those allowances. Your kids need to know the timeframes in order to make their lists. Once the lists are complete, you're ready to determine the allowance amounts.

Don't feel obligated to give your children $50 a week in spending money if that's what the worksheet shows. The amount you give is your decision based on the amounts you're giving now, what you can afford and what you feel is appropriate. If you do decide to give less, you may need to help your children trim down their financial responsibilities so they have a shot at making a go of it.

2.    Next, review and discuss each set of money challenges with your child. As they master each challenge, have them color in or check off the circle next to that challenge.

A common theme in all the challenges is "Plan It! Do It! Review It! and Stick To It!". If the challenges seem a little advanced for your children, you may want to just emphasize the Plan It! Do It! Review It! and Stick to It! idea of keeping up with their money.

3.    Finally, make your children aware of your policies on matching, transfers and advances and let them know when you intend to do the next review.

⭐ Please note the *Kid's Money Wizard Journal* is addressed to your children and is intended to be read, discussed and completed by the two (or three) of you. You may notice we alternate using the he and she pronouns in the Money Wizard descriptions. We hope this doesn't cause any confusion. Enjoy this time with your children as you watch your little he's and she's become big-time Money Wizards!

# KID'S MONEY WIZARD JOURNAL

## PLANS, CHALLENGES, & POTION

# SPENDING
## MONEY WIZARD

> *A Spending Money Wizard knows how much she has available to spend and what she needs to spend it on. She knows her funds are limited and often makes tradeoffs between two things she would really like. She compares price and quality and always gets value for her money. A Spending Money Wizard is comfortable with her decisions and confident with her skill.*

## THE POTION & THE PLAN

Getting The Potion right is essential for the magic to happen. The Spending Amount must be reasonable to you and your parents. It needs to be specific and written. This worksheet helps you do both.

Start by making a list of everything your parents are either buying for you or giving you the money to buy. Our list will help you get started. Check the items you want to include. Cross out the ones you don't. Write additional items on the blank lines.

Figure the cost of each item and how often it's purchased over the allowance period. In other words, if you're getting $2 every day for snacks and your allowance period is one week, multiply 2 times 7 and put the resulting $14 next to snacks.

These amounts need to include sales tax as applicable. If your parents buy you one CD a week that costs $12.95 and the sales tax is 9.25% (as it is in Tennessee), put down $14.15 as the cost of a CD.

List any item you get less often than each allowance period on the Saving page. For example, if you get one used video game every month and the allowance period is one week, divide the $20 cost (which should include sales tax) by 4 and write $5 for that one video game in your Saving Allowance.

Don't leave anything out. Sometimes it's hard to think of each and every item. It may be helpful to make this list over a period of days or even weeks. Take the time to do it right. Once you start receiving your allowance, it's harder to add items.

Once your list is complete, add up all the items and put the total in the Spending Amount boxes. Don't automatically assume you're getting this amount. It's merely a starting point for your discussion with your parents.

# Spending Money List / Plan

| | | | |
|---|---|---|---|
| ◯ Candy | $ [ ][ ] . [ ][ ] | ◯ Make-Up | $ [ ][ ] . [ ][ ] |
| ◯ Sodas | $ [ ][ ] . [ ][ ] | ◯ Nails | $ [ ][ ] . [ ][ ] |
| ◯ Snacks | $ [ ][ ] . [ ][ ] | ◯ Hair Styling | $ [ ][ ] . [ ][ ] |
| ◯ Toys | $ [ ][ ] . [ ][ ] | ◯ Tanning | $ [ ][ ] . [ ][ ] |
| ◯ Comic Books | $ [ ][ ] . [ ][ ] | ◯ Jewelry | $ [ ][ ] . [ ][ ] |
| ◯ Action Figures | $ [ ][ ] . [ ][ ] | ◯ Car Insurance | $ [ ][ ] . [ ][ ] |
| ◯ Games | $ [ ][ ] . [ ][ ] | ◯ Gasoline | $ [ ][ ] . [ ][ ] |
| ◯ Trading Cards | $ [ ][ ] . [ ][ ] | ◯ _____ | $ [ ][ ] . [ ][ ] |
| ◯ Dolls | $ [ ][ ] . [ ][ ] | ◯ _____ | $ [ ][ ] . [ ][ ] |
| ◯ Doll Clothes | $ [ ][ ] . [ ][ ] | ◯ _____ | $ [ ][ ] . [ ][ ] |
| ◯ Video Games | $ [ ][ ] . [ ][ ] | ◯ _____ | $ [ ][ ] . [ ][ ] |
| ◯ CDs | $ [ ][ ] . [ ][ ] | ◯ _____ | $ [ ][ ] . [ ][ ] |
| ◯ Videos/DVDs | $ [ ][ ] . [ ][ ] | ◯ _____ | $ [ ][ ] . [ ][ ] |
| ◯ Clothes | $ [ ][ ] . [ ][ ] | ◯ _____ | $ [ ][ ] . [ ][ ] |
| ◯ School Supplies | $ [ ][ ] . [ ][ ] | ◯ _____ | $ [ ][ ] . [ ][ ] |
| ◯ Sporting Goods | $ [ ][ ] . [ ][ ] | ◯ _____ | $ [ ][ ] . [ ][ ] |
| ◯ Magazines | $ [ ][ ] . [ ][ ] | ◯ _____ | $ [ ][ ] . [ ][ ] |
| ◯ Books | $ [ ][ ] . [ ][ ] | ◯ _____ | $ [ ][ ] . [ ][ ] |
| ◯ Movies | $ [ ][ ] . [ ][ ] | ◯ _____ | $ [ ][ ] . [ ][ ] |
| ◯ Sporting Events | $ [ ][ ] . [ ][ ] | ◯ _____ | $ [ ][ ] . [ ][ ] |
| ◯ Concerts/Plays | $ [ ][ ] . [ ][ ] | ◯ _____ | $ [ ][ ] . [ ][ ] |

Spending Amount  $ [ ][ ] . [ ][ ]

**Parents**—As soon as you decide how much allowance you will provide for Spending, add your decision to The Potion.

After you've done that, have your child revise the list so the Spending Amount is less than the Allowance Amount. She may need to delete items and reduce individual amounts. When she's done, the list becomes her Spending Money Plan.

## The Challenges

Once you get The Potion right, all you need to do to become a Spending Money Wizard is to master The Seven Spending Money Challenges:

○ Challenge #1 — Plan Your Spending
○ Challenge #2 — Make Your Own Decisions
○ Challenge #3 — Plan Your Shopping
○ Challenge #4 — Keep Receipts
○ Challenge #5 — Limit Your Spending
○ Challenge #6 — Shop For Value
○ Challenge #7 — Review Your Plan

**#1 Plan Your Spending.** Review your list of responsibilities and make sure it reflects how you want to spend your money. Add and delete items as appropriate. Realize you can only spend your money once. If you choose to buy something not on your list, decide which item on your list you're not going to buy.

**#2 Make Your Own Decisions.** Don't let your spending be influenced by television and magazine ads, store displays, sales, coupons or friends. To assure you're happy with all your decisions, always decide on your own what is best for you. If you're just not sure, ask someone whose opinion you value and consider what they have to say.

**#3 Plan Your Shopping.** When you go to the store, know what you're going to buy. Promise yourself you're not going to get anything else. If you find something you like, work it into your Spending Plan and buy it on a future trip. It may also be helpful to take only the money you need for the purchase you plan to make. Extra cash has a way of finding unplanned purchases.

**#4 Keep Receipts.** There's no sweat when you return something if you have the receipt. If you paid cash, you get your cash back. If you put it on a check card, you get credit to your account. Even if the item's been marked down, you still get back exactly what you paid. Without a receipt, you get the marked-down price and generally a store credit instead of the cash. Decide where you're going to keep your receipts and always put them there. An envelope, small box or drawer is a good possibility.

**#5 Limit Your Spending.** Running out of cash can put you in a bind. Try not to spend every dime you get. Unexpected items always come up. Try to have some cash left at the end of the allowance period. That way, if all your friends decide at the last minute to go to a movie, you're able to afford a ticket, too.

**#6 Shop For Value.** If you live close to a discount or outlet store and can find the item you need at a reduced price, buy it there. The same goes for using sales, coupons and bulk purchases to your advantage. Get the best price you can locally for the things you need to buy. Don't get caught driving across town and spending a dollar in gas to save $.20 on a candy bar or using a $5 off coupon to buy something you don't really need.

You can also get value by going generic. Brand names are generally quite costly. If the quality is the same, save some money and buy the generic item. Used items offer much the same value.

Don't be fooled by huge discounts on inflated prices. In other words, that $300 necklace for $60 could really be a $25 piece of jewelry. Learn what a fair price is for a particular item by shopping around. Determining value can be especially challenging when shopping over the Internet or from catalogs. Items are often made to look like more than they actually are. Always try to make sure you're getting real value for your money.

**#7 Review Your Plan.** If you're running short of cash and can't figure out the problem, try keeping a running total of how much spending money you have left. Start by writing down the allowance amount. Every time you buy something, deduct it from the total. That way, you know at the time you're considering a purchase if it will leave you with enough money to make it until the next allowance. If it doesn't, you might want to put off that purchase.

If you still can't figure out the problem, keep a log of everything you spend for the entire allowance period. At the end of that time, see how much of your spending is not in your plan and adjust your spending or your plan accordingly. If you can't decide which item to cut, try numbering the items in your plan from the most important to the least important. Cross off the least important ones until your plan looks like it's going to work.

Your parents may have more thoughts on Spending Money Challenges. Ask them and add their suggestions here:

_____

_____

_____

_____

_____

_____

_____

# SAVING
## MONEY WIZARD

> *A Saving Money Wizard knows he has more wants than he can cover with a single allowance. He knows he must set aside a certain portion of his income, on a regular and recurring basis, to be able to satisfy them. A Saving Money Wizard pays himself first. That way, he's always assured of reaching each and every one of his saving goals.*

## THE POTION

Your regular allowance is the total of your Spending, Saving and Sharing amounts. At this point, all you have is the Spending amount and the Saving and Sharing percentages. To get the Saving amount, you need to do the following calculations:

100 %

— ☐☐ % Saving

1) Figure the Spending percentage by subtracting the Saving and Sharing percentages from 100%.

— ☐☐ % Sharing

☐☐ % Spending

2) Figure the Allowance amount by dividing the Spending amount by the Spending percentage.

$☐☐.☐☐   Spending amount

/  .☐☐   Spending percentage

$☐☐.☐☐   Allowance amount

3) Figure the Saving amount by multiplying the Allowance amount by the Saving percentage.

$☐☐.☐☐   Allowance amount

* .☐☐   Saving percentage

$☐☐.☐☐   Saving amount

Add this result as the Saving amount in THE POTION.

## ⚡ The Challenges ⚡

Once you get The Potion right, all you need to do to become a Saving Money Wizard is to master The Five Saving Money Challenges:

○ Challenge #1 — Plan Your Saving
○ Challenge #2 — Safeguard Your Funds
○ Challenge #3 — Set Aside The Money
○ Challenge #4 — Refine Your Plan
○ Challenge #5 — Supercharge Your Saving

⚡ **#1 Plan Your Saving.** The best way to make sure you reach your Saving Goals is to write them down. Make a list of the things you want to save for and how much you need for each one. Put those goals you can reach quickly in the short-term column and those that will take more time in the long-term column.

Our list will help you get started. Check the items you want to include. Cross out the ones you don't. Write additional items on the blank lines.

If your parents are matching your Saving, reduce the total needed by the amount they have agreed to provide. For instance, if you need $600 for a school trip and your parents are matching $1 for $1, you need to save $300. You would write down "School Trip" and put $300 as your Saving Goal. Once you've set the goal, write down how much you will save from each allowance to achieve it.

⚡ **#2 Safeguard Your Funds.** You don't want to raid your savings to buy something not on your list. If you really can't live without some special something, go ahead and make it a Saving Goal. If you can't wait to have it, put more or even all of your Saving Allowance towards that item. Whatever you do, don't blow the money you've worked so hard to save on some whim.

One way to avoid raiding your savings is to make it as hard as you can to get to it. Keeping that money anywhere around the house is way too handy. Open one no-fee Savings account at

your local bank or credit union for each Saving Goal. Get a register to help you keep up with each account. If you can only get one no-fee account, have your parents help you set up a ledger sheet to record your individual progress towards each goal.

⚡ **#3 Set Aside The Money.** Deposit your money in your Savings account as soon as you get your allowance. Divide it between the items on your saving list and record each deposit amount in your registers or ledger. Always remember to pay yourself first. It's the most important bill you'll ever have!

⚡ **#4 Refine Your Plan.** The time it takes to save for something gives you a chance to think about that purchase. As the money's building up in your savings, you may decide you no longer want that particular item. No problem. Just cross it out and move the money to the other items. You'll reach those goals that much faster.

⚡ **#5 Supercharge Your Saving.** Use money you don't spend from your Spending Allowance, cash you receive as gifts and money you make from odd jobs to reach your Saving Goals even faster. That way, you'll turn your dreams into realities more quickly than you ever imagined.

Your parents may have more thoughts on Saving Money Challenges. Ask them and add their suggestions here:

⚡ _____

_____

⚡ _____

_____

## Short-Term

○ CD       $ ☐☐
    Each Allowance    $ ☐.☐☐

○ Concert Ticket    $ ☐☐
    Each Allowance    $ ☐.☐☐

○ Trip Money    $ ☐☐
    Each Allowance    $ ☐.☐☐

○ _____    $ ☐☐☐
    Each Allowance    $ ☐.☐☐

## Long-Term

○ Trip       $ ☐☐☐☐
    Each Allowance    $ ☐.☐☐

○ Laptop PC    $ ☐☐☐☐
    Each Allowance    $ ☐.☐☐

○ Car       $ ☐☐☐☐
    Each Allowance    $ ☐.☐☐

○ _____    $ ☐☐☐☐
    Each Allowance    $ ☐.☐☐

RECOMMENDED FOR AGES 5+

# SHARING
## MONEY WIZARD

*A Sharing Money Wizard knows she can make a difference in the world by giving of her time and money to causes she believes in and to those less fortunate. She takes a set amount of everything she gets and dedicates it to sharing with others.*

## THE POTION

Your regular allowance is the total of your Spending, Saving and Sharing amounts. At this point, all you have is the Spending and Saving amounts and the Sharing percentage.

Figure the Sharing amount by multiplying the Allowance amount by the Sharing precentage.

$ ☐☐.☐☐    Allowance amount

\*     .☐☐    Sharing percentage

$ ☐☐.☐☐    Sharing amount

Add this result as the Sharing amount in THE POTION.

## THE CHALLENGES

Once you get The Potion right, all you need to do to become a Sharing Money Wizard is to master The Three Sharing Money Challenges:

○ CHALLENGE #1 — PLAN YOUR SHARING

○ CHALLENGE #2 — SET ASIDE THE MONEY

○ CHALLENGE #3 — STICK TO YOUR PLAN

# Sharing Money Challenges

⚡ **#1 Plan Your Sharing.** Start by listing the recurring needs you have for Sharing. Our list will help you get started. Check the items you want to include. Cross out the ones you don't. Write additional items on the blank lines.

For example, you may go to church every week and donate a dollar to the offering. Or, you may attend a monthly meeting that involves a contribution. Whatever the group or activity, add the name, the total contribution and the amount you will need to set aside from each allowance. If you donate $1 a week to church and $4 every month to another group, you would list $1 per week for church and $1 per week for the other group.

Next, list one-time needs. For instance, you may have an annual fundraiser at school that requires a $26 donation or you may want to donate $13 to the Salvation Army's annual fund drive. On a weekly basis, that's $.50 for school and $.25 for the Salvation Army. While you're at it, you might as well build in a little cushion for that unexpected donation. Something is always bound to come up. Another $.50 a week may be a good amount.

In this example, you've come up with $3.25 a week for Sharing. If you're allowance Amount is $3 a week, you need to make some adjustments. Another way to go about setting your Sharing Goals is to start with the Allowance Amount and divide it up the best you can among the Sharing needs you have.

⚡ **#2 Set Aside The Money.** Each time you get your allowance, divide it between the items on your Sharing list. Do it just like you were paying a bill. Use an envelope, jar, piggy bank or any other convenient place to keep your Sharing money.

⚡ **#3 Stick to Your Plan.** You may be tempted to spend some of your Sharing money on yourself. Don't! Have the discipline to put it where it's going to do the most good—for yourself and for others.

Your parents may have more thoughts on Sharing Money Challenges. Ask them for their suggestions.

# Sharing Money Plan

**Recurring**

○ Church

Each Allowance

$ ☐ . ☐☐
$ ☐ . ☐☐

○ _____

Each Allowance

$ ☐ . ☐☐
$ ☐ . ☐☐

○ _____

Each Allowance

$ ☐ . ☐☐
$ ☐ . ☐☐

**One-Time**

○ School Fund Drive

Each Allowance

$ ☐☐ . ☐☐
$ ☐ . ☐☐

○ _____

Each Allowance

$ ☐☐ . ☐☐
$ ☐ . ☐☐

○ _____

Each Allowance

$ ☐☐ . ☐☐
$ ☐ . ☐☐

# GiFT
## MoNeY WiZard

A Gift Money Wizard knows friendships aren't measured by the amount spent on a gift. He knows a thoughtful present, recognizing the true interest of a close friend, always means more than a very expensive gift he'll seldom enjoy. Knowing the limit on allowance funds and the amount of sacrifice and work in providing additional money makes reasonable spending the Gift Money Wizard's m.o. (modus operandi).

## The Challenges

To become a Gift Money Wizard you must first master The Three Gift Money Challenges:

○ **Challenge #1 — Restrain Your Generosity**

○ **Challenge #2 — Plan Your Purchase**

○ **Challenge #3 — Shop For Value**

**#1 Restrain Your Generosity.** Remember the strength of the friendship is not determined by the cost of the gift. Sometimes, an expensive gift can put the other person in an awkward position. They may be concerned they won't be able to afford a similarly priced gift when it's their turn to buy one for you.

**#2 Plan Your Purchase.** Decide how much you want to spend and what you want to buy. If you already have a gift in mind, it's simply a matter of coming up with the money. On the other hand, if you only have so much money to spend, it's a matter of coming up with the gift. Either way, taking the time to plan before you go shopping avoids the overspending that often comes when you make a decision at the store.

**#3 Shop For Value.** Once you've made your decision, try to get the best value for your money, just like you'd do for any other purchase. Now's the time to summon your Spending Money Wizard for help.

Your parents may have more thoughts on Gift Money Challenges. Ask them and add their suggestions here:

_____

_____

_____

_____

_____

_____

# CLOTHES
## Money Wizard

*A Clothes Money Wizard knows the difference between fads and fashion. She knows how much money she has to spend and everything she needs to buy. She recognizes true value in items she can wear more than one season. Sales and coupons are helpful tools when she uses them to buy the things on her list.*

### The Potion & The Plan

Getting The Potion right is essential for the magic to happen. The Clothes Allowance must be reasonable to you and your parents. It needs to be specific and to be written. This worksheet helps you do both.

Start by making a list of all the clothing items you need for the allowance period. For instance, if your allowance is for the six months from September through March, list all the Fall and Winter clothes you need. From April through August, list all the Spring and Summer clothes you need. Try to think of everything from socks to hats.

Our lists will help you get started. Check the items you want to include. Cross out the ones you don't. Write additional items on the blank lines. For you convenience, we've provided lists for all four seasons. If you get a semi-annual allowance, simply complete the appropriate two lists.

Once your list is complete, add up all the items and put the subtotal in the boxes provided. Then, multiply that amount by your local sales tax rate and enter the tax amount in the next set of boxes. To arrive at the total needed for Clothes, simply add the subtotal to the tax amount.

Don't automatically assume that's what you're getting. It's merely a starting point for your discussion with your parents.

Remember, this is more of a wish list than a shopping list. Expect your parents to adjust and eliminate items. They may have a maximum amount they're able to spend. If so, rework the list so the total does not exceed that amount. They may also have thoughts on the necessity of certain items or the cost associated with them. Finalizing the Clothes List usually requires some give and take between you and your parents.

Once you have an amount, this page becomes your Clothes Money Plan. That doesn't mean you'll buy each and every item and nothing else. The only thing set in stone is the amount and the fact it's got to last for the allowance period. How you spend it is up to you. The list is one way you can make it work. If you come up with another way, you may want to put it on paper first to make sure you can afford it. Trying to keep up with it in your head is a lost cause.

www.AllowanceMagic.com

# Clothes Money Lists/Plans

## Spring Clothes

- ○ Casual Shoes $ ☐ ☐ ☐
- ○ Athletic Shoes $ ☐ ☐ ☐
- ○ Jackets $ ☐ ☐ ☐
- ○ Slacks $ ☐ ☐ ☐
- ○ Shorts $ ☐ ☐ ☐
- ○ Shirts $ ☐ ☐ ☐
- ○ Pajamas $ ☐ ☐ ☐
- ○ Swimwear $ ☐ ☐ ☐
- ○ Jeans $ ☐ ☐ ☐
- ○ Underwear $ ☐ ☐ ☐
- ○ Socks $ ☐ ☐ ☐
- ○ T-Shirts $ ☐ ☐ ☐
- ○ _____ $ ☐ ☐ ☐
- ○ _____ $ ☐ ☐ ☐
- ○ _____ $ ☐ ☐ ☐
- ○ _____ $ ☐ ☐ ☐
- ○ _____ $ ☐ ☐ ☐
- ○ _____ $ ☐ ☐ ☐
- ○ _____ $ ☐ ☐ ☐
- ○ _____ $ ☐ ☐ ☐

Spring Subtotal $ ☐ ☐ ☐

Sales Tax + $ ☐ ☐

Spring Total $ ☐ ☐ ☐

## Summer Clothes

- ○ Casual Shoes $ ☐ ☐ ☐
- ○ Athletic Shoes $ ☐ ☐ ☐
- ○ Jackets $ ☐ ☐ ☐
- ○ Slacks $ ☐ ☐ ☐
- ○ Shorts $ ☐ ☐ ☐
- ○ Shirts $ ☐ ☐ ☐
- ○ Pajamas $ ☐ ☐ ☐
- ○ Swimwear $ ☐ ☐ ☐
- ○ Jeans $ ☐ ☐ ☐
- ○ Underwear $ ☐ ☐ ☐
- ○ Socks $ ☐ ☐ ☐
- ○ T-Shirts $ ☐ ☐ ☐
- ○ _____ $ ☐ ☐ ☐
- ○ _____ $ ☐ ☐ ☐
- ○ _____ $ ☐ ☐ ☐
- ○ _____ $ ☐ ☐ ☐
- ○ _____ $ ☐ ☐ ☐
- ○ _____ $ ☐ ☐ ☐
- ○ _____ $ ☐ ☐ ☐
- ○ _____ $ ☐ ☐ ☐

Summer Subtotal $ ☐ ☐ ☐

Sales Tax + $ ☐ ☐

Summer Total $ ☐ ☐ ☐

# Clothes Money Lists/Plans

## Fall Clothes

- Casual Shoes $ [ ][ ][ ]
- Dress Shoes $ [ ][ ][ ]
- Coats $ [ ][ ][ ]
- Slacks $ [ ][ ][ ]
- Sweaters $ [ ][ ][ ]
- Skirts $ [ ][ ][ ]
- Pajamas $ [ ][ ][ ]
- Dresses $ [ ][ ][ ]
- Jeans $ [ ][ ][ ]
- Underwear $ [ ][ ][ ]
- Socks $ [ ][ ][ ]
- _____ $ [ ][ ][ ]
- _____ $ [ ][ ][ ]
- _____ $ [ ][ ][ ]
- _____ $ [ ][ ][ ]
- _____ $ [ ][ ][ ]
- _____ $ [ ][ ][ ]
- _____ $ [ ][ ][ ]
- _____ $ [ ][ ][ ]

Fall Subtotal $ [ ][ ][ ]
Sales Tax + $ [ ][ ]
Fall Total $ [ ][ ][ ]

## Winter Clothes

- Casual Shoes $ [ ][ ][ ]
- Dress Shoes $ [ ][ ][ ]
- Coats $ [ ][ ][ ]
- Slacks $ [ ][ ][ ]
- Sweaters $ [ ][ ][ ]
- Skirts $ [ ][ ][ ]
- Pajamas $ [ ][ ][ ]
- Dresses $ [ ][ ][ ]
- Jeans $ [ ][ ][ ]
- Underwear $ [ ][ ][ ]
- Socks $ [ ][ ][ ]
- _____ $ [ ][ ][ ]
- _____ $ [ ][ ][ ]
- _____ $ [ ][ ][ ]
- _____ $ [ ][ ][ ]
- _____ $ [ ][ ][ ]
- _____ $ [ ][ ][ ]
- _____ $ [ ][ ][ ]
- _____ $ [ ][ ][ ]

Winter Subtotal $ [ ][ ][ ]
Sales Tax + $ [ ][ ]
Winter Total $ [ ][ ][ ]

**Parents**—As soon as you've decided how much allowance you will provide for Clothes, add your decision to THE POTION.

After you've done that, have your child revise the list so that the total of the items is less than the Allowance amount. She may need to delete items and reduce individual amounts. When she's done, the list becomes her Clothes Money Plan.

## THE CHALLENGES

Once you get The Potion right and you've mastered the seven Spending Money Challenges, all you need to do to become a Clothes Money Wizard is to master Two Clothes Money Challenges:

○ CHALLENGE #1 — BATTLE BRANDS
○ CHALLENGE #2 — FIGHT FADS

**#1 Battle Brands.** A brand name, supported by a multi-million dollar promotional campaign, doesn't necessarily mean a better product. All you can be sure of is it's more expensive. Be selective in purchasing brand name fashions. You'll probably be limited as to what you can afford. You may need to restrict yourself to only one or two brand name products and get store brands for the rest.

**#2 Fight Fads.** It's almost impossible to get your money's worth out of clothes you can only wear for a month or two. Stretch your dollars by buying clothes you'll still be happy to wear next year. Get more for your money by shopping clearance items as the seasons change. Both your wardrobe and your pocketbook benefit.

Your parents may have more thoughts on Clothes Money Challenges. Ask them and add their suggestions here:

_____

_____

_____

_____

_____

_____

_____

_____

# The Potion

## The Potion

**Parents**—This is where you record each decision you've made in the previous sections. Collectively, these decisions shape the allowance program. Each item defines a particular aspect of that program. Making your own decisions insures your program reflects your family's values as well as each child's individual needs and capabilities. Once you've filled in all the blanks, all you need to do is stick to it and watch The Potion work its magic!

**Draw a line through the arrows of the transfers you choose not to allow:**

| Transfers | | |
|---|---|---|
| Spending | → | Saving |
| Spending | → | Sharing |
| Spending | → | Clothes |
| Spending | → | Gift |
| Saving | → | Spending |
| Saving | → | Sharing |
| Saving | → | Clothes |
| Saving | → | Gift |
| Sharing | → | Spending |
| Sharing | → | Saving |
| Sharing | → | Clothes |
| Sharing | → | Gift |
| Clothes | → | Spending |
| Clothes | → | Saving |
| Clothes | → | Sharing |
| Clothes | → | Gift |

**Write in the amounts and frequencies of the allowances you decide to give:**

| Allowance | % | Amount | Frequency |
|---|---|---|---|
| Spending | | | |
| Saving | | | |
| Sharing | | | |
| Total | | | |
| Clothes | | | |
| Gift | | | |
| Friends | | | |
| Family | | | |

**Check the boxes indicating your decisions:**

| Match Savings From: | Matching Rate: |
|---|---|
| ☐ Saving Allowance | ☐ $2 For $1 |
| ☐ Spending Allowance | ☐ $1 For $1 |
| ☐ Earnings | ☐ $.50 For $1 |
| ☐ Cash Gifts | ☐ _____ |

| Advances | ☐Yes  ☐No |
|---|---|

**Fill in the agreed upon date:**

| Next Review Date | / / |
|---|---|

## Stay The Course

- Keep The Challenges before you and The Potion true.

- Be relentless in the pursuit of your objectives.

- Achieve Money Wizardry and enjoy financial prosperity.

- TAW

| Today's Date |
|---|
| / / |

# MORE MAGIC

Additional copies of *Allowance Magic* can be ordered from Kids' Money Store on the Internet at kidsmoneystore.com, through the mail at P.O. Box 681861, Franklin, TN 37068-1861, by phone at 615-790-7233 or by Fax at 615-790-2394. Visa and MasterCard are accepted for payment on all orders. Checks and money orders are also accepted on mail orders. Do not send cash. For your convenience, an order form is provided below.

| Quantity | Item | Price | Total |
|---|---|---|---|
| ____ | **ALLOWANCE MAGIC** TURN YOUR KIDS INTO MONEY WIZARDS | $8.95 | _____ |

Ship To

_____
Name

_____
Street or P.O. Address

_____
City, State, ZIP

| | |
|---|---|
| Subtotal | _____ |
| Sales Tax[1] | _____ |
| Shipping[2] | _____ |
| Total | _____ |

[1]Applicable only to shipments to Tennessee addresses at a rate of 9.25%

[2]Shipping Charges:
Postal Book Rate     $3.00[3]
Priority Mail          $5.00[3]
Next Day Air          $20.00[3]

[3]Rates are for shipments to U.S. addresses only and are subject to change without notice.

Indicate payment method:

○ Visa  **VISA**
○ MasterCard  **MasterCard**
○ Check
○ Money Order

For credit card payments:

Card Number _____ Name on Card _____

Expiration Date ____ / _____ Signature _____